RAINBOW
MOON
TAROT

SAMANTHA WEST

T0405414

ROCKPOOL

A Rockpool book

PO Box 252
Summer Hill
NSW 2130
Australia

rockpoolpublishing.co

Follow us! f ⊙ rockpoolpublishing
Tag your images with #rockpoolpublishing

ISBN: 9781925946819

Published by Rockpool Publishing in 2022
Copyright text and images © Samantha West, 2022
Copyright design © Rockpool Publishing, 2022

Cover and text design by Daniel Poole, Rockpool Publishing

Printed and bound in China

10 9 8 7 6 5 4 3 2 1

CONTENTS

The Minor Arcana
CUPS

WANDS

CRYSTALS

DAGGERS

INTRODUCTION

T he *Rainbow Moon Tarot* was born out of a desire to see a diverse group of bodies in tarot while still maintaining a magical and whimsical energy. When I began this project in 2018, I knew representing real bodies was the most important part of the puzzle, so I put out a call on Instagram for volunteers. The support was completely overwhelming, and suddenly this personal little project took on so much more meaning.

I received an outpouring of requests from people who wanted to see bodies like theirs, so I reviewed the hundreds of volunteers and selected as many diverse bodies as I could, including many influential voices in the online tarot community.

THE GENDER BINARY AND TAROT

The gender binary has always been a big part of tarot. We hear a lot about masculine and feminine energy. But as we get more comfortable with breaking those boundaries as a society, it may be time to get more comfortable reframing the gender binary in tarot. This deck has no gendered cards. They have been renamed to reflect their meanings without the genders attached.

HOW TO READ TAROT

READING STYLES AND ETHICS

Reading tarot cards is a personal journey that is unique to every reader, and how you choose to approach it is entirely up to you. This book covers the basic meanings of the cards, and it follows the Smith Rider Waite tradition, the classic and best-known tarot tradition. This version consists of 22 Major Arcana and 56 Minor Arcana cards.

If you're beginning your tarot journey, there are a couple of core questions to ask yourself when picking up your deck.

WILL I READ FOR OTHER PEOPLE?

Many readers choose to only read for themselves, some read for those close to them and others sling cards for anyone. When I began my tarot journey, I read only for myself out of fear of how my family and friends would react, and of feeling embarrassed in front of them. Once I began reading for others, my connection with the tarot deepened and I found my calling as a reader. Don't ever feel pressured to do something you're not comfortable with – follow your own path.

WHAT ARE MY ETHICS?

Figuring out your ethics as a tarot reader is an ever-evolving process. There are no concrete rules and as you figure out your way, you'll hit roadblocks that make you feel uneasy. Some examples include reading for pay, pulling cards for people who are not present, previous-life readings, and love readings. It may be helpful to keep a notebook and jot down the things that make you feel uncomfortable.

SPREADS

Spreads are how we lay out the cards in order to answer our questions. The most common 'spread' is a single-card pull. At the beginning of your day, sit and reflect on your plans. Now, ask your card an open-ended question – a question that can't be answered with a simple 'yes' or 'no'. For example, we wouldn't ask the cards 'Will I enjoy this trip?' Instead, we'd ask 'How can I make the most of this trip?' I also like to phrase my questions as asking for advice, as opposed to being predictive. For example, instead of asking 'What will today be like?' I'll ask 'What energy should I bring to today to make it the best possible day?'

Reading is personal and unique to every reader, but here are a couple of spreads to help get you started!

LOVE BLOCK

Great for communication issues in any kind of relationship.

BLIND SPOT

What is preventing you from getting to the truth?

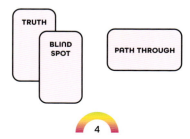

MAJOR ARCANA

The Major Arcana are the big lessons and major themes in our lives. When a Major Arcana card appears in your reading, this is the strongest message the cards have to tell you, so listen carefully.

– 0 –

FOOL

New beginnings; fresh start

The Fool is at the beginning of the journey. Like a newborn, they are naive and ignorant of everything to come. They're starting afresh with nothing but potential. Pack your bags and take a deep breath: you're about to start a completely new journey. This is a time for a leap of faith – you may not know what's to come, but that can be when the best adventures happen! Enter this new journey with the self-awareness that you don't have all the answers, and keep an eye out for any dangers that may present themselves.

- I -

MAGICIAN

Readiness; equipped with the correct tools

The magician has all their tools right in front of them and knows how to use them. You've done everything you can to prepare; you've equipped yourself with everything you could possibly need. If you're hesitating about taking the next step, don't. You're ready; you've prepared for this. Own your talents! You're more gifted than you give yourself credit for.

– II –

DIVINE

(Also known as the High Priestess)

Intuition; instinct; collective unconscious

The Divine is just that – *divine*. Heavenly and otherworldly, they have strong intuition and know everything that's going on behind the curtain. This is a card about trusting your intuition and looking inward before taking action. The Divine is comfortable in their seat and is patient, and this is a time for you to be the same. Things will come to light. This is not a time for outward energy but a time to look inward. We've all been gifted with divine intuition, and you're being called to quiet all the outside voices and listen to what your gut is telling you.

– III –

CREATOR

(Also known as the Empress)

Creative; receptive

The Creator is a nurturing, indulgent energy; they radiate abundance and creativity. This is a call for receptive energy: self-care, love and nurturing. Connect with yourself and the earth around you. The Creator is also just what their name says – a maker, and an artist. This card can mean it's time to lean into your creativity and put something out into the world. The Creator is often associated with fertility, but that can mean so much more than the birth of a child, such as the creation of a new invention, business or work of art.

- IV -

AUTHORITARIAN

(Also known as the Emperor)

Boundaries; structure

The Authoritarian is the opposite of the Creator –
they represent structure and power. They are a leader
who embraces a consistent, deliberate life. This card tells
you it's time to find some structure; to find comfort in
knowing your own boundaries and allowing yourself to
carve out space. Don't be afraid to lay out your
boundaries and demand they be respected.

- V -

ROOTED

(Also known as the Hierophant)

Teacher; guide; tradition

The Rooted is the gatekeeper of tradition, deeply rooted in the environment in which they were raised. They are a mentor or teacher, passing on everything they've learned. It may be time to find someone or something to teach you. Don't be afraid to reach out and find a guide or do the work to become your own teacher. This is a call to open up and learn – allow yourself to be led.

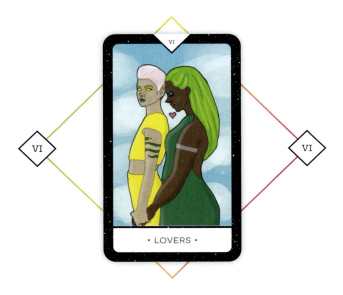

- VI -
LOVERS

Duality; big choices

The Lovers are about duality and relationship.
This does not necessarily mean a romantic relationship;
rather, the relationship between any two entities.
This is often an indication of a big choice! Both sides
have value and need to be weighed carefully. When this
card pops up in a relationship reading, it's calling for a
well-balanced partnership, not a lusty romance.

- VII -
CHARIOT

Momentum; movement; urgency

The Chariot is all about movement and momentum!
This is the time to grab the reins and drive forward.
If you've been holding yourself back, it's time to
move forward. Reach for the stars. This card represents
truly going the distance and not holding yourself back.

– VIII –
STRENGTH

Spiritual strength; resilience

When we think of strength, we often think of brutal physical strength. But this card represents our internal strength – our resilience and our control. The person on this card is not fighting the lion, but has tamed it, just as you have the power to control yourself. You have the power within to face your fears, stand up for yourself and be heard.

- IX -
HERMIT

Solitary; alone; withdrawing

The Hermit adventures alone, using their lantern to find a way for themselves. They're not relying on anyone else to guide them, and they've found comfort in their own company. It's time to take some time to yourself – take a step back from your surroundings and the people you normally surround yourself with. Spend some time with your own thoughts and find guidance within yourself.

- X -

WHEEL of FORTUNE

Change in fate

The Wheel of Fortune is here to remind us our fate
is not always in our own hands. If you're looking for an
answer, it may be time to release and let the universe take
its course. Everything is already in motion and you can't
change that, so it's time to let go and watch how everything
falls. This card also often represents a change in fortune, so
if you've been down on your luck, things may start looking up!
However, if you've been on a winning streak, it may be time
to prepare yourself for a rough patch.

- XI -

JUSTICE

Balance; fairness; equality

Justice holds the scales tightly, indicating a need for balance. It's time to consider what is truly fair. You need to look at yourself and your situation through objective eyes: how can you restore balance to the situation? This may also be an indication that balance is coming; whether you're ready or not, justice is going to be served. Have you been wronged by someone? They may be about to get what is coming to them. On the other hand, have *you* wronged someone? Time to own up and face the consequences.

- XII -
HANGED

Change in perspective; suspension

The Hanged is upside down, but is not in distress.
They're here by choice. They've flipped themselves
over on purpose, and now they're seeing things from a
new perspective. Release the tension and relax into this
new position for a breath. Get comfortable taking on a
perspective that isn't your usual one. Take a moment of
suspension, but don't stay there too long.

- XIII -
DEATH

Transformation; release

Death is transformation. We don't disappear when
we die; we go from one state of being to the next.
This card indicates an ending, release or transformation.
Death can be scary, but it is a part of life. This isn't to
dismiss the trauma that death can bring. Take a moment
to mourn the loss and then release it. You need to release
things in order to make room for something new. You can't
move on if you're holding onto the past.

- XIV -
TEMPERANCE

Harmony; balance

Temperance is living a peaceful existence – balanced;
harmonious. Things are falling into place: you're finding
harmony with those around you and with your environment.
You're adapting to your surroundings and, most importantly,
you're learning to trust the universe. The universe has
your back! Divine intervention is on the horizon.

- XV -
DEVIL

Addiction; internal struggles; cycles of harm

The Devil has chains, but they aren't tangling or constricting; they are simply offered to us. The Devil doesn't lunge at us or demand anything. They know we'll put those shackles on ourselves. The Devil is all about the cycles we chain ourselves to – addictions, bad behaviours. This is a call to take a good long look at your situation and what you're chaining yourself to. Throw off the chains and break the cycle!

- XVI -
TOWER

Rock bottom; pain; struggle

Everything is on fire! Okay, not really, but it probably feels that way. Things are really bad, but they need to be bad – you need to hit rock bottom. You're letting everything burn to the ground so you can start something fresh. It may feel like a loss right now, but this has happened to make room for growth. You can rebuild from the ashes. Let it all fall, and make sure you take notes – learn from this loss so next time you can build on stronger foundations.

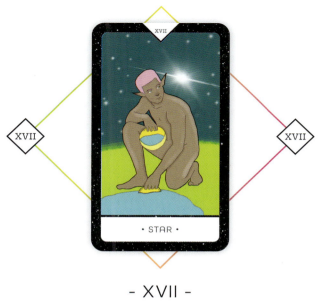

– XVII –
STAR

Self-care; luxury

The Star is living their best life – taking care of themselves in a beautiful environment. The Star is about embracing self-care; taking in the warmth after a cold night. You've been through some stuff, and it's time to focus on you. Make sure your body and soul find nourishment, because we're no good to anyone else if we're not doing good for ourselves.

– XVIII –
moon

Shadow; darkness; secrets

The Moon represents the darkness – our shadow selves.
These are all the things we don't bring into the light and may
not be ready for others to see. This is a time for introspection
and self-work. Take some time to work through your shadows.
Allow yourself to explore the dark, intrusive thoughts you
wouldn't want others to know. In knowing our darkness,
we know our true selves. The Moon also represents
secrets – all the things we keep in the dark.

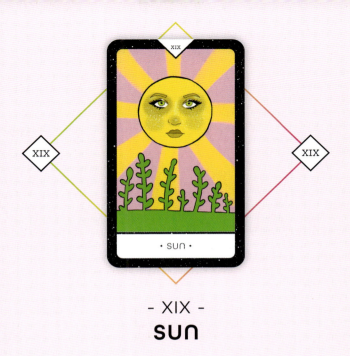

- XIX -
SUN

Clarity; truth; light

The Sun brings everything to light – good and bad.
This is a time of true, radiant clarity. It often comes
as our 'aha!' moment, when everything suddenly
becomes clear. Take a moment to absorb all the truth
you're seeing, celebrate the good things and acknowledge
any negatives that have come to light.

- XX -
JUDGEMENT

Self work; bias

Judgement is calling for you to review yourself:
to contemplate your biases and work on releasing things
that are keeping you from becoming your higher self.
Look at what is holding you back – any pettiness, or
judgement you're holding for others is likely just self-doubt at
play. Work on yourself, forgive yourself, and move up. You'll
only achieve the best possible version of yourself if
you acknowledge all sides of who you are.

- XXI -
WORLD

Completion of a cycle

The World is the last card in the Major Arcana and
represents everything coming to completion. You have
survived the cycle and can now sit back and benefit from
all your hard work. Take some time to contemplate
everything you've learned, take note of anything you could
have improved on, and bring those lessons with you moving
forward. Give yourself a moment to breathe and celebrate
everything you've accomplished and survived.

MINOR ARCANA

Each suit in the Minor Arcana
represents a different area
of our lives. Note that within
each suit, Chancellors have
replaced Queens and Wardens
have replaced Kings.

CUPS

Cups represent our heart and emotions

ELEMENT: WATER

ACE of CUPS

A new emotional beginning; a renewal of
self-love; the spirit is overflowing

The Ace of Cups is a new beginning of the heart.
You are open and ready for a new love or a new
connection, and the universe hears your call.
Prepare yourself for a beautiful and emotional ride.

TWO of CUPS

TWO of CUPS

*A new romance; blossoming love; balance within
the relationship; kindred spirits*

A new love is blooming, and it's a beautiful thing!
You've found a partner or companion who fills your cup
as much as you fill theirs. This is such a healthy balance,
and it's important to maintain that for a long-lasting and
fulfilling relationship. Enjoy every moment of this love.

THREE of CUPS

THREE of CUPS

Friendship; soul connections; surrounding yourself with people who balance you

It's a rare occurrence to find people who understand us inside and out. Our friends can be the family we choose for ourselves, giving us the love we need. You've found your people and it's important to appreciate everything they bring to your life.

FOUR of CUPS

Focus on yourself and your own achievements.
Avoid a wandering eye and jealousy

You are finding yourself swamped with opportunities for
growth but you're content with where you are right now.
Taking a beat to appreciate everything you already have
instead of constantly grasping for the next rung on the ladder
can be important for emotional health and growth.

FIVE of CUPS

FIVE of CUPS

*Sadness; grief; loss; struggling with moving on:
time to focus on healing*

There has been an emotional loss, and this is not a
push to move on. This is a call to feel what you need to feel,
and heal. There is no timeline for grief, so allow yourself
room to mourn what you've lost. Take a step back and focus
on yourself. Attempting to force yourself through the grief
process will just prolong your suffering.

SIX of CUPS

SIX of CUPS

Nostalgia, childhood, family, ancestral baggage:
what can be gained by reflecting on the past?

Memories of childhood bring up different emotions for
different people. For some it brings a sense of nostalgia
and innocence; for others it can induce anxiety and uproot
memories of trauma. The Six of Cups calls for you to take a
moment, look back on your childhood and see what lessons
you can bring from your experiences. It may even be time
to look further, towards your ancestral lineage, and see what
generational trauma may need healing.

SEVEΠ of CUPS

SEVEΠ of CUPS

Overwhelmed by choices; head in the clouds:
time to ground ourselves

If there's one thing you're not lacking, it's choices. You have every possible avenue laid out in front of you so it's time to stop procrastinating and choose a path. This isn't a time to daydream or explore the what-ifs, it's a time to ground yourself and make a logical and balanced decision.

EIGHT of CUPS

EIGHT of CUPS

Inability to release the past and forgive:
move on to a higher calling

You are finding yourself unable to find joy in your current situation. No matter how hard you try to find the spark that once brought you here, it cannot be reignited. It may be time to release what's no longer serving you. It's hard to let go of something you once loved, but remind yourself the past is not what defines you. The present is not serving you, so it's time to release and move on to your higher calling.

NINE of CUPS

NINE of CUPS

Fertility and success; joy; contentment

You've worked so hard and you've come so far. Everything is falling into place around you. It's okay to smile and do a little happy dance – all the things you've been wishing and praying for are coming true. Don't let this moment escape you, and don't allow yourself to self-sabotage. This is true joy and happiness – and you deserve it.

TEN of CUPS

TEΠ of CUPS

Long-lasting happiness; happily ever after; joy in relationships and on a spiritual level; beyond the physical

Happily Ever After. This is true contentment. This is not the kind of happiness that's fleeting, but the kind that burns inside you for a long time. This is the joy that comes from a relationship that's been built on trust and open communication over years, and that has found comfort in each other's quiet company. This isn't a lustful love, but a deep, friendship-based love that lasts a lifetime.

PAGE of CUPS

Dreamer; flighty; new opportunities

The Page of Cups is a dreamer. They have their
head in the clouds – and a short attention span
to match. They dream of new beginnings and
new opportunities for us. At the moment, these are
just ideas. How can you bring them into reality?

KNIGHT of CUPS

KNIGHT of CUPS

Romantic; call to action

The Knight of Cups is a gentle romantic – they want
to share their love with the world, and help others
see the bright side of things. The Knight of Cups wants
you to take your dreams and desires and be inspired
to channel them into action.

CHANCELLOR of CUPS

CHANCELLOR of CUPS

Listener; instinctive

The Chancellor of Cups is the ultimate receptive
energy – they're a wonderful listener and
sounding-board. They call for you to take a moment
and trust your heart. You know the truth within you.

WARDEN of CUPS

WARDEN of CUPS

Emotional balance

The Warden of Cups is a mentor and healer:
they take care of everyone around them, but make
sure to maintain a strong balance of heart and mind.
The Warden of Cups calls on you to maintain balance
and maturity in any issues that may arise, and to
look out for those around you.

WANDS

Wands represent our creativity and passions

ELEMENT: FIRE

ACE of WANDS

New ideas and creative potential

There's a spark of an idea that's popped into your mind.
It may be a new piece of art, a business idea or an invention.
You keep seeing it in your mind's eye, and you know it has
potential to be something great. Don't ignore that spark.
Don't talk yourself out of pursuing it. Make time to explore
this idea and see how far it can take you.

TWO of WANDS

TWO of WANDS

*Creative partnership or a choice: time to take the
next step and start something new*

A new project has taken root in your life and it's time
to take it to the next level. This means making room for
it in your schedule and really giving yourself the chance
to see its potential, then taking the next big leap.

THREE of WANDS

THREE of WANDS

*Potential for growth; shedding things
you've outgrown and moving up*

You've been working hard on your project.
It's taking up room in your life and you're giving it
everything you have. Release anything that isn't working.
Don't allow yourself to be hung up on the things that failed,
but focus on growing everything that is going well.

FOUR of WANDS

FOUR of WANDS

Celebrations; events: take a moment to
appreciate yourself and your work

Hooray! It's time to celebrate! You're hitting a big milestone,
and it's time to take a minute to lift your nose from the
grindstone and bask in everything you've accomplished.
This can be a celebration of any kind – work, personal,
relationship, family – just know that it's time to PARTY!

FIVE of WANDS

FIVE of WANDS

Chaotic; disorganised; unfocused; at strife

Ouch. Things are rough right now. There's strife, with fighting and chaos all around you. So much dust has been kicked up, it's hard to see clearly. Nothing can come into focus right now. Try to find your way out of battle to catch your breath before making any big decisions.

SIX of WANDS

Dwell on the positive: look at the goodness in the situation; appreciate what you have

You work so hard and you're being acknowledged for your accomplishments. People are starting to take notice of everything you've done, and it's okay to allow yourself a moment in the spotlight. This is a big milestone and it deserves some attention. Take a moment to look back and see how far you've come and how much growth you've accomplished. Take a beat to dwell on it before jumping to the next milestone.

SEVEN of WANDS

SEVEN of WANDS

You'll have victory through courage:
face your obstacles head on

You've worked hard to get as far as you have, but you're
not at the finish line quite yet. You're hitting a barricade,
but don't let that stop you. This isn't the time to give up.
Face your opponent head on with a strong strategy. You're too
bright to wing it, so make sure you attack with precision
and purpose. You have what it takes to win.

EIGHT of WANDS

EIGHT of WANDS

*Act quickly: something new is going to cross
your path – don't miss the opportunity*

The eight of wands calls for us to jump into action.
A new opportunity has popped up and this isn't a
time to pause and weigh your options – it won't wait.
Act quickly before it disappears, because you'll kick
yourself if you miss it.

NINE of WANDS

NINE of WANDS

Stay on course: this struggle will pass,
and you'll be stronger because of it

It feels like you've lost the battle *and* the war.
You've worked so hard, and you're beaten to the
bone by everything life has thrown at you. But you're
almost there. The finish line is just over the hill, and you
have everything it takes to make it. So give yourself one
last hard push – you'll be so glad you did!

TEN of WANDS

TEN of WANDS

*Overburdened; overwhelmed: time to re-evaluate
and solve what can be solved*

You are carrying the weight of the world on your
shoulders. You've carried everything from beginning
to end and it's weighing you down. But it's important to
remember why you picked up this load to begin with, and
remind yourself why you decided it was worth it.

PAGE of WANDS

PAGE of WANDS

Passion; new opportunity

The Page of Wands is someone who brings passion –
they are excited for the new opportunities that are
in front of them. They are enthusiastic and high energy.
This can also represent excitement about a new
creative opportunity on the horizon.

KNIGHT of WANDS

Goal-driven; impulsive

The Knight of Wands pursues their goals unapologetically.
This drive and passion make them charismatic and
attractive to others. Be wary of being too impulsive and
consider the impact on those around you.

CHANCELLOR of WANDS

CHANCELLOR of WANDS

Manifestation; balance

The Chancellor of Wands holds a lot of power and
has the ability to manifest what they truly desire.
They are a well-balanced and grounded force who
see their projects through to the end.

WARDEN of WANDS

WARDEN *of* WANDS

Leader; delegator

The Warden of Wands is passionate and focuses
on their work. They stand behind their projects and are
highly regarded for it. They are a natural leader and help
guide those around them to a common goal. They aren't
afraid to delegate and play to the strengths of their team.

CRYSTALS

Crystals represent the physical realm,
for example money and possessions

ELEMENT: EARTH

(Previously Pentacles)

ACE of CRYSTALS

An opportunity – a seed to plant, with unlimited potential

A new opportunity has popped up – possibly a financial
investment. Think of this as a seed: planted, it has unlimited
potential, but it will need a lot of tending in order to grow.
Put time and consideration into where the seed will go,
and how it will best thrive before planting it.

TWO of CRYSTALS

TWO of CRYSTALS

Juggling tasks and maintaining balance

You're playing a game of juggling, and maintaining
balance is important. You have multiple tasks that
all require equal attention and care. Be sure to give all
sides of your life the attention they deserve, because
that balance is key to your happiness.

THREE of CRYSTALS

THREE of CRYSTALS

Teamwork; working to each member's strength

You can't accomplish everything on your own: sometimes you need to lean on your teammates in order to achieve success. Be a good teammate and do your fair share, and make sure everyone is playing to their individual strengths. This isn't a time to take the wheel and dominate – it's a time to listen and work together.

FOUR of CRYSTALS

FOUR of CRYSTALS

Greed; only focused on material gain; scarcity

The fear of loss and going without is your driving
force in pursuing your goals, and that's not a long-term
solution. It will lead to burnout. Greed is turning you sour.
You're currently sitting on your riches, afraid to share.
Reach into your pockets and share, and you may find it
more rewarding than all the money in the world.

FIVE of CRYSTALS

FIVE of CRYSTALS

Financial hardship, lost opportunities and unemployment

You've hit hard times. Money is tight, and you've lost
out on opportunities. It's okay to feel not okay right now.
Things are stressful, and you may not be sure how you're
going to navigate through this. This is not a time to take a
gamble. Save what you can, when you can, in order to survive.

SIX of CRYSTALS

Sharing; harmony; well-deserved rewards

You've worked hard for all you've earned, but that doesn't mean much unless you have someone to share it with. If the opportunity arises to help someone out of a bad situation, offer a hand. We enter these agreements in good faith, not expecting a return on our investment beyond the good it brings to someone else.

SEVEN of CRYSTALS

SEVEN of CRYSTALS

Financial responsibility; investment; hard work

You're working hard for every penny earned.
You put a lot of blood, sweat and tears into everything
you do, and sometimes it doesn't feel like it's worth it –
but don't give up. You're going to see a return on
everything you've put in, and then some.

EIGHT of CRYSTALS

EIGHT of CRYSTALS

Pride in a life well fought for; learning a new trade or skill

You've chosen a path you want to pursue –
it's time to master a new skill. Work hard to learn the
ins and outs of your trade or craft. Take the time to
really learn everything there is to offer. Don't give up
when things get tough – this is a skill worth learning.
Take on a mentor or guide to help you navigate,
and take pride in everything you learn.

NINE of CRYSTALS

Solitary success; enjoyment in the good things

Take a moment to bask in all the luxury you've
acquired through your hard work. You may not be living
in a mansion on a private island, but you've built a
comfortable life and it's time to soak in all that has to offer.
Indulge yourself a bit – you've earned it!

TEN of CRYSTALS

TEN of CRYSTALS

Wealth; all your hard work has paid off;
acquiring something large

You have worked so hard for so long – and you're
achieving all your goals. You're finally going to have a
chance to breathe, and bask in all you've accomplished.
The Ten of Crystals also appears when you may be
receiving an inheritance – the culmination of
generations of work and saving.

PAGE of CRYSTALS

PAGE of CRYSTALS

New financial opportunity; pursuit of goals

The Page of Crystals is a bringer of new beginnings founded strongly in the material realm. They are calling for you to build on your professional or physical dreams – to start aiming for those goals. Be practical, and be tactical.

KNIGHT of CRYSTALS

KNIGHT of CRYSTALS

Planning; steadfast; hard worker

The Knight of Crystals calls for us to be
practical when reaching for our goals. Set out a clear
plan and stick to it. There's a lot of hard work ahead
– slow and steady wins this race.

CHANCELLOR of CRYSTALS

CHANCELLOR of CRYSTALS

Balance of home and work

The Chancellor of Crystals is the master of balancing
work and home: they know where their priorities lie,
and when one side should outweigh the other. The Chancellor
of Crystals works hard to provide for their loved ones.
They are guiding you to find balance in your life.

WARDEN of CRYSTALS

WARDEN of CRYSTALS

Master of field

The Warden of Crystals has worked hard for
everything they have – they've become the master
of their industry. They are here to acknowledge all your
hard work – you've done exactly what you set out to do,
and you should relish that.

DAGGERS

Daggers represent our brains,
thought processes and intellect

ELEMENT: AIR

(Previously Swords)

ACE of DAGGERS

ACE of DAGGERS

A new way to use your mind – a new idea; an epiphany

A new idea has popped into your mind!
Or possibly a new approach to something. You've been
thinking about things the same way for such a long time,
a different method might be exactly what you need.
This may come as a moment of clarity or an epiphany.

TWO of DAGGERS

Small mental block; self-suppression; a bind we have put on ourselves; imbalance

You're having a complete mental block – you're unable
to see what may be clear to others. Take a breath and
try to approach the problem from a different angle.
You may feel frustrated, but it's important to remember
that this problem is coming from within. You have everything
you need to take off the blindfold and tackle the issue.

THREE of DAGGERS

THREE *of* DAGGERS

Heartbreak; deep emotional pain that bleeds
into the rest of our life; wreckage

Complete and utter heartbreak. The Three of Daggers
feels like three actual daggers stabbing us through the heart.
This is the kind of damage that can wreck us for a
long time. The cards aren't calling for you to take action;
they're calling for you to be gentle with yourself.
This is an acknowledgement of your pain.

FOUR of DAGGERS

FOUR of DAGGERS

A call to rest; lay down arms, stop fighting

You've been fighting so hard. Everything feels tough right now and while you may have more fight left in you, now is not the time. Reserve your energy and lay down your weapons. This is a time to rest.

FIVE of DAGGERS

Fighting; self-harm; failure

You've fought hard – but was it worth it? All this turmoil has made its way inside you and you're walking away feeling broken. Has anyone really won here? Was it worth all the pain it caused? Is there even any repairing the damage that was done? This doesn't come with an easy fix – just some lessons to take moving forward.

SIX of DAGGERS

SIX of DAGGERS

Step away from the situation, you've been fighting a losing battle; beginning a journey to something better

It's time to move on. Pack up everything, say goodbye to all that isn't serving you and let go. This is a time to release all that baggage that's been weighing you down. Let go of the toxic thoughts that take up space in your mind. Get out of situations that aren't bringing you anything in return.

SEVEN of DAGGERS

SEVEN of DAGGERS

Dishonesty; lying; defeat; secrets; trickery;
something behind the curtain

Oh, there is some sneakiness happening here.
Someone thinks they are getting away with a big lie,
but everything comes to light eventually. This card comes
when we're being told to take a second look at something
that isn't quite adding up. Is someone lying? Are *you* lying?
Remember: nothing stays hidden forever.

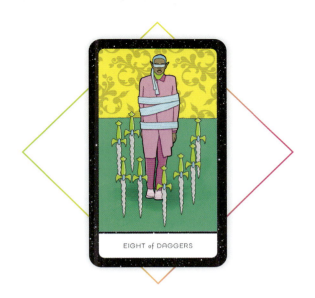

EIGHT of DAGGERS

EIGHT of DAGGERS

Paralysed from fear; inability to move; helpless

You feel like you're completely trapped. Everything feels
out of your control and you can't take the next step.
But you can. You are so much more capable than you're
giving yourself credit for. You are not a victim – you are
strong, and you have everything you need to move forward.
It's time to open your eyes.

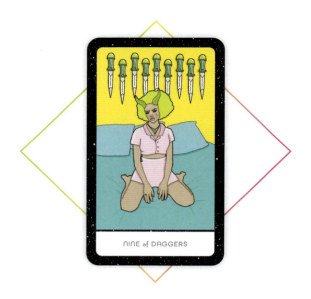

ΠΙΠΕ of DAGGERS

Anxiety; tension; stress; suffering; illness; loss

Darkness is creeping in. Things feel bad, and your
mind is working against you. Anxiety and nightmares may
be taking hold of you. It may feel as though you are spiralling
– one bad thing leads to another. The Nine of Swords is
telling you that you are not a victim of your own mind – do
what you must in order to break the chains. This may be a
call to take a break, or take care of your mental health.

TEN of DAGGERS

Rock bottom: take a moment to mourn and learn from this, rest, then move forward

We've all heard the famous last words, 'Well, it can't get any worse!' Then everything immediately does get worse! Don't worry – this really is rock bottom. On the bright side, you can only go up from here. Take a moment to grow from this: how did you get here? What could you have done differently? Take a rest, then get back up and brush off the dirt. If you're not dead, it's time to move on.

PAGE of DAGGERS

PAGE of DAGGERS

Student; learning and growing

The Page of Daggers has a thirst for knowledge: they are
a young student, eager to learn and prove themselves.
They call for you to learn, too – it may be a new
way of thinking or communicating.

KNIGHT of DAGGERS

KNIGHT of DAGGERS

Ambition; advocate

The Knight of Daggers is fast-moving. They are ambitious, acting swiftly with a lot to prove. They call for you to work for what you want, communicate clearly and advocate for yourself.

CHANCELLOR of DAGGERS

CHANCELLOR of DAGGERS

Boundaries; clear communication

The Chancellor of Daggers is the ruler of
boundaries and communication. They've honed these
skills and are not afraid to use them. They call for you to
make sure you're respecting your own boundaries and
communicating clearly with those around you.

WARDEN of DAGGERS

Truth; unbiased; clear thoughts

The Warden of Daggers is a speaker of truth.
They have worked through the issue, and have a
clear, unbiased mind. They call for you to do your
research, and then speak the truth as well.

ABOUT THE AUTHOR

S amantha West was born and raised in New Jersey, USA. She grew up with a love of art and creating things with her hands. Her mother encouraged her to pursue any avenue that interested her, and that led to her experiencing all forms of art. She was gifted her first tarot deck when she was 15, and her journey as a witch grew from there. Artwork became interwoven with her spirituality. As she got older, she received a master's degree in Interior Architecture, but always felt called back to the freer forms of artwork. She found her calling when she began working on her first tarot deck in 2018, and has continued creating and helping others bring their visions to life ever since. She is now a full-time illustrator who teaches a course on tarot deck creation. When she isn't drawing, she can be found knitting or making candles with her husband and baby girl.